# fast
# thinking:
# team
# meeting

**PEARSON EDUCATION LIMITED**

Head Office:
Edinburgh Gate
Harlow CM20 2JE
Tel: +44 (0)1279 623623
Fax: +44 (0)1279 431059

London Office:
128 Long Acre
London WC2E 9AN
Tel: +44 (0)20 7447 2000
Fax: +44 (0)20 7240 5771
Website: www.business-minds.com

First published in Great Britain in 2001

ISBN 0 273 65314 8

*British Library Cataloguing in Publication Data*
A CIP catalogue record for this book can be obtained from the British Library

Typeset by Pantek Arts Ltd, Maidstone, Kent.
Printed and bound in Great Britain by Ashford Colour Press, Hampshire

*The Publishers' policy is to use paper manufactured from sustainable forests.*

# fast thinking: team meeting

- ▶ keep your focus
- ▶ motivate your team
- ▶ achieve your goals

by Ros Jay

# contents

**introduction**     6

**fast thinking gambles**     10

**1: your objective**     12
Why are you holding this meeting?     14
The social side     15
Preparing meetings at short notice     16

**2: the agenda**     20
The agenda items     22
Ordering the agenda     24
Adding the detail     26
      Information     28
      Action     29
      Decision     29
Allocating time     32

**3: involving other people**     36
Providing back-up     38

**4: chairing the meeting**     42
Structure     43
Keeping to time …     48
Minutes     52

## 5: handling people 56

Servant not master 57

The ground rules 58

Handling aggression 60

    Let people let off steam 62

    Be neutral 63

    Involve the rest of the group 64

    Keep to the facts 66

Control the dominant tendency 66

Be positive 68

    Set the right tone 69

    Don't settle for the first solution 70

    Be creative 72

Reaching consensus 73

## 6: the type of meeting 76

Regular departmental meetings 77

    Why are we here? 78

Inter-departmental meetings 79

Project meetings 81

Team briefing sessions 83

    Monitoring 84

    The briefing 85

## team meeting in ten minutes 88

# introduction

So which team meeting is it this time? Project team? Inter-departmental meeting? Team briefing? Whatever it is you need time to prepare for it effectively – but what time? You meant to start planning for it days ago, but somehow the work caught up with you (doesn't it always?) – probably even overtook you – and you're down to your last few minutes. The meeting is in an hour and you haven't started thinking about it yet. Until now.

What you need is a brief guide (definitely brief) to planning and running effective team meetings on the hoof. Well, you got it. This book contains everything you need to know to plan and prepare for your meetings. And once you get to the meeting, you can't afford to waste time. You need to run meetings that occupy the minimum time so you can get on with your life. And of course they need to be truly productive: it's hard enough scheduling the time in the first place, without wasting it when you get there.

This book is about preparing and running team meetings. You could argue that any meeting by its nature is a team meeting. It is attended by several people who, for the purposes of the meeting, are working together as a group. But the phrase 'team meeting' implies that the members of the group also work together outside the meeting, as a department or a project team, or at least in the same organisation. This is the assumption you will find in this book. (Mind you, almost exactly the same rules apply to chairing any other meeting.)

Most team meetings, though not all, are regular. However, this doesn't mean to say that the preparation you did for the last meeting will do for this one. The advance work needs doing afresh each time. And you may well feel that your regular meetings are always hampered by being underprepared, running too long or being unproductive. You want to do something about it, but you don't have time to go on seminars or read long books on management practice. You simply want:

 **tips for looking as if you know more than you do**

 **shortcuts for doing as little preparation as possible**

 **checklists to run through at the last minute**

... all put together clearly and simply. And short enough to read fast, of course.

Let's suppose your meeting is tomorrow. In your dream world you would have finished preparing your meeting by now. The agenda, in all its detail, would have been circulated ten days ago, and you'd have blocked out in your diary a relaxing couple of hours this afternoon to go through all the background papers thoroughly. Before the meeting tomorrow you've allowed 15 minutes to get into the right frame of mind and think through the key results you expect from this meeting.

*Wake up!* This is the real world, and you'll be lucky if you make it to the meeting on time, and luckier still if you get 30 seconds before it to remember where you are. That's why this book will take you through the whole process fast, with a section at the end for preparing the meeting in ten minutes if you're working at the speed of life.

So take a deep breath, and relax. It's all in here, and by the time you've worked through this book your meeting will be planned and prepared, and you'll be ready to get through it with lightning efficiency and maximum productiveness. What's more, you'll also find all the information you need to do the job when the heat is off (just in case that ever happens).

This book will take you through the five key steps of preparing and running a team meeting:

1  Begin by setting the objective for the meeting so that you can be faster and smarter in your planning and execution.

2  The next stage is to prepare the agenda – more than simply scrawling a list of items for discussion, a well-prepared agenda will make the meeting far quicker and more productive.

3  Now you need to involve the other people by circulating the relevant paperwork.

4  After this comes the task of chairing the meeting itself; we'll begin by looking at the practical skills you need so your meetings can be halved in time and doubled in effectiveness.

5  People skills are equally important when it comes to getting the most out of your meetings, so we'll look at these too.

Finally, we'll look at the particular guidelines for specific types of team meetings:

▶ regular departmental meetings
▶ inter-departmental meetings
▶ project meetings
▶ team briefing sessions.

This book will take you through the five key steps of preparing and running a team meeting

# fast thinking gambles

The accepted thinking is that you should leave longer to prepare for team meetings (although the accepted thinking doesn't seem to have thought about how you're supposed to find the time). The idea is that you can't plan and run meetings effectively under time pressure. But is this really true?

So long as you are acting smart as well as fast, there's no reason why you shouldn't run team meetings that are better than those most of your colleagues run, even when you're spending only half the time on them. But there are disadvantages to meetings at breakneck speed. Here are some of the key ones:

- If the agenda is not prepared well in advance, it won't be circulated well in advance. This means that the other participants may not have time to prepare fully (you're not the only one with more work than time, you know). Missing information and ill-prepared arguments do nothing for the productiveness of meetings.

- If you are pushed for time, you may well not get around to reading all the background papers before the meeting (surely not?). Appearing ill-informed about the content of your own meeting does nothing for your credibility, quite apart from diminishing the effectiveness of the meeting.

- Problems and conflicts can arise at meetings, which are easier to handle if you have allowed time to think about them in advance and prepare for them.

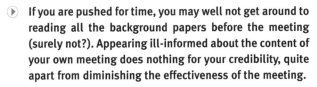

Fast thinking will ensure that your team meetings are professional, speedy and effective. But you'll always have a better chance of getting the most out of the time you spend in meetings if you start preparing well in advance. So always aim to give yourself a good run up to a meeting. Failing that, trust to fast thinking.

# 1 your objective

An objective? For a meeting? And we've just established that time is short. We haven't got time to mess about with objectives, surely? Well yes, we have got time and I'm afraid it's got to be done. But before you slam the book shut in annoyance and write it off as another waste of money, just let me explain.

Objective setting can help make your meetings faster. You see, once you know what your objective is, you can see which of your agenda items meet it and which don't. And often, you can scrub the ones that don't. There, that's starting to sound more like fun. In fact, sometimes you can scrub whole meetings if they don't help to further your objective. Yep, just like that. Cancelled. Go away everyone, we're not having a weekly meeting this week. Find something else to do instead.

I hope that makes objective setting seem more worthwhile. Of course, much of the point is to make sure that the meeting achieves what it sets out to (by defining just what it *does* set out to do). But it is also important in this fast-moving age to avoid wasting time on anything else. So you need to start the process with a clear objective.

Almost without exception, the objective of the meeting as a whole will be the objective of the team, for example:

- ▶ **to ensure that this project is successfully completed on time and on budget**
- ▶ **to build company profits and customer satisfaction**
- ▶ **to keep the running costs of the organisation down and productivity up**
- ▶ **to ensure that this department meets its targets.**

That is why you are holding the meeting, and you need to keep sight of your objective. It should take only a couple of minutes to phrase it; when you have done so, write it down. One of the first things we tend to do when we are in a hurry is stop thinking. But a few moments' thought now will save you plenty of time later. What's more, if this is a regular meeting, you won't have to go through this every time. The objective of the monthly team meeting will always be the same; you will simply need to remind yourself of it each month.

Once you know what your objective is, you can see which of your agenda items meet it and which don't

## TIME OUT

Make yourself stop everything until you have identified your objective. Time yourself for three minutes and don't allow yourself to do anything else in this time. That way, you can't be tempted to skip this bit just because you're up against the clock.

Once you have a clear objective you can view each suggested agenda item in the light of it – as we'll see later. If the item does not help the meeting to achieve its objective, it may well not belong there at all. Of course it may still need attention, but perhaps in informal discussion, exchange of e-mails or memos or at a separate meeting.

### WHY ARE YOU HOLDING THIS MEETING?

Most regular meetings are held for the same reason: because it's the weekly/fortnightly/monthly meeting so we hold it every week/fortnight/month. But do you really need to? If holding the meeting doesn't further the team's objective in any way, why hold it? The first question you should ask when you plan a meeting is: 'Do we really need this meeting at all?' If the answer is no, cancel the meeting. It's your meeting, after all – you can do what you like. You haven't got the time to hold meetings that you don't need:

- ▶ **Perhaps you usually need the weekly meeting, but you could skip it this week.**
- ▶ **Maybe you could switch your fortnightly meetings to monthly meetings, or the weekly meeting to a fortnightly one.**

### THE SOCIAL SIDE

Although cancelling unnecessary meetings is often the best course, it is worth being aware that team meetings do have an important social function. Sometimes it is worth holding a meeting more frequently than you might, or face-to-face rather than on the phone, in order to reap the social benefits:

**PICK UP THE PHONE**

Could you replace your meeting with a conference call? These tend to be much quicker. Regular meetings can sometimes alternate a face-to-face meeting with a phone meeting to save time.

- ▷ **It establishes and reinforces the identity of the team.**

- ▷ **It reinforces each person's role in the team, from their place in the hierarchy to the value of their contribution (including reinforcing your position as leader of the team).**

- ▷ **It establishes collective commitment and responsibility – decisions arrived at democratically are more likely to be supported by everyone, even those who didn't vote for them.**

So don't hold a meeting just for the social side – a team drink down the pub after work might do the job just as well – but do bear it in mind as a point in favour of holding a meeting rather than cancelling it.

### PREPARING MEETINGS AT SHORT NOTICE

Let's be frank. You cannot run a truly polished and professional meeting at an hour's notice. This is because you should have circulated the agenda at least a week ago. You can certainly do the preparation in an hour and often far less, but not now. Last week.

The agenda needs to be circulated to give everyone time to read any background papers, and collect any information they want to present to the meeting, or find the figures to back up their view on an important agenda item. It also gives people time to get back to you if they feel strongly that another item should be included or an existing one should be deferred until the following meeting.

Without this opportunity, you may well find that time is wasted at the meeting because people haven't mugged up on the background to an item, or vital information is missing without which you can't take the decision you wanted to. Or people try to argue about what should or shouldn't be on the agenda.

So what can you do about it now? Well, you have three options:

1 My best advice is: postpone this meeting if you possibly can, even for just three or four days. You may even be able to cancel it altogether if it is a regular meeting with no urgent items to discuss. Use the time you have set aside now to prepare and circulate the agenda, and hold the meeting once everyone has had time to read and act on it.

2 Failing this, hold a brief meeting to cover only those agenda items that simply cannot wait. Defer anything else until the next meeting.

3 If you must hold the meeting, you must. But promise yourself you'll start planning earlier next time (and a promise is a promise ... isn't it?)

Remember, you don't need any more time to prepare well for a meeting. You need the same time, only sooner. So before the next meeting:

▸ Ask for any background papers you need for circulation in reasonable time for people to submit them (often you will ask for them at the previous meeting).

▸ Prepare the agenda a week to ten days ahead of the meeting (or three days for a regular weekly meeting). Block this time in your diary well in advance. In fact, for regular meetings, you could go through your diary now and mark in the time for the rest of the year.

▸ Circulate the agenda, with all the necessary background papers, in plenty of time – remember, most of your colleagues have more work than time, too.

Remember, you don't need any more time to prepare well for a meeting. You need the same time, only sooner

# 2 the agenda

Most people write pretty pathetic agendas, if the truth be told. They are little more than a list of items to discuss. I suppose that's better than nothing, but really it is only an aide-mémoire to make sure you miss nothing out.

The genuine article, however, will make your meeting faster, more productive and clearer for everyone. It will avoid confusion and time-wasting, and ensure that each item achieves a concrete end result. You'll be able to zap through your meetings, scattering results, decisions and action points all around you as you go.

To indicate the value of a proper agenda, it might help to remind you what can happen with one of those list things that so often passes for an agenda. How often do any of the following happen in meetings?

- You spend 20 minutes debating which of two proposals to accept: the pricey or the cheaper option. The cost of those 20 minutes – in terms of the value of your time and everyone else's – far exceeds the cost saving you are debating.

- You spend half an hour discussing an agenda item but reach no conclusion, and have to discuss it all over again another time.

- You discuss next year's targets for 15 minutes, and then spend three quarters of an hour haggling over the new car park allocation of reserved spaces.

- Someone turns up without the necessary information to feed into the meeting because they misunderstood the agenda item. For example, when it said 'NEC exhibition' they assumed it meant the scheduling was being discussed, so they didn't bring the quotes and draft designs for the stand.

- You come away from the meeting still unable to get on with certain tasks because the meeting never made the decision you were hoping for.

Well the good news is, such time-wasting and inefficiency is now a thing of the past, at least in your meetings. A clear, well-planned agenda means your team meetings will be swift, time will be allocated effectively and items will have a purpose – no more vague discussion that leads nowhere. So how is it done?

### THE AGENDA ITEMS

The first step is to establish which topics should be on the agenda. You'll have a mental list, no doubt, and perhaps requests from other people. The other key source of agenda items is the minutes from the last meeting (assuming this is not a one-off meeting). This may well stipulate certain action points to be completed in time to feed into this meeting.

Once you have your list of items, the most common problem at this stage is finding that your list is too long. A regular team meeting shouldn't really run much longer than an hour – people have neither the time nor the concentration to do it justice. A project team or inter-

**thinking smart**

#### MEETING YOUR OBJECTIVE

Check all the agenda items against your objective to make sure they belong in the meeting. Eliminate any that don't belong there – perhaps they should be discussed or agreed outside meeting time by a smaller group of people or maybe one person alone can take charge of them rather than waste the meeting's time.

departmental meeting might need longer, but shouldn't go beyond two hours, as a rule of thumb. You're trying to keep this meeting short and your list of items is fighting you all the way. So if you need to slim down the agenda, here are a few tips:

- If this agenda is looking longer than usual, hold over any non-urgent items to the next meeting (of course, this doesn't work if your agenda is bound to be this long next time, too).

- See if any items can be covered by a sub-group. Either they can have decision-making authority, if necessary, or they can feed into the main meeting without the whole debate having to be repeated.

- It can be easier to schedule, and more productive in the long run, to hold more than one meeting. Not everyone will have to attend both if you plan them sensibly, which will also help speed them up (small meetings are always quicker than large ones).

- Some agenda items are generally for information only. We'll look at these in more detail later, but often they don't need to take up meeting time at all – they can simply be circulated as a document and the item can be cut from the agenda.

## NO OTHER BUSINESS

One of the best ways to save time at meetings is to ban 'any other business' from the agenda – it is an invitation to people to dream up things to discuss for the sake of it. It is also sometimes used by schemers as a ruse to spring items on the rest of the meeting for Machiavellian purposes, knowing that no one else has prepared for them. Occasionally you can allow a request to add a last-minute item when there is good reason, but don't invite it.

### ORDERING THE AGENDA

The next stage is to put the agenda items into a logical order. This doesn't just mean the most important item goes first: your meetings aren't going to overrun so everything will get discussed for the appropriate amount of time. Here are several useful tips for ordering the agenda as effectively as possible:

▷ **Really urgent items should be near the top of the agenda. Your meetings may run on time, but there's always the chance the building will catch fire or some other unforeseen happening will halt the meeting.**

- Sometimes one item will depend on the outcome of another, and this will affect the order. For example, there's no point discussing the schedule for the NEC exhibition until you've established whether you are definitely going to attend it.

- It makes sense to group related items together so that people don't have to make too many huge mental leaps during the meeting.

Those are the logistical considerations, but there are also psychological factors that affect the ordering of the agenda:

- People tend to be more wide awake and creative at the start of a meeting, so any items that will need bright ideas and inventive thinking are best off near the top of the agenda.

- An attention lag sets in after about 15 or 20 minutes, so that's a good place for any hot topic that people are capable of getting animated about, even at this stage.

- Some items will unify the group, while others will divide it. Be aware of this when you draw up your agenda. You may want to start by unifying the group before you introduce the more controversial topics, or you might prefer to do things the other way around. But be aware of which you are doing, because it makes a difference to the mood of the whole meeting.

### UNITED WE STAND

Whatever order you choose for the items that bring the team together or divide it, you should always end with an item on which everyone is united – preferably against a common cause. This might be anything from another department to new legislation; the point is that it will strengthen team spirit as everyone leaves the meeting.

ADDING THE DETAIL

What you have now isn't yet an agenda; it's still just a list of topics to discuss. Now you need to turn it into an agenda. And you do that by fleshing out the detail. An agenda needs clarity more than it needs brevity. It doesn't matter if your agenda runs to two or even three pages, so long as it helps everyone to understand what the meeting is about.

That's not to say you should write an essay under each topic. In any case you haven't got time for that. But you should make it clear what aspect of the topic is in the spotlight, otherwise people won't be able to prepare effectively for the meeting. So instead of putting simply: 'New brochure'; it is far more helpful to put: 'To discuss the format of the brochure in the light of the

26

budget and costings' – and then attach the costings, of course. Otherwise most people won't know whether you're discussing the format, the design, the content or the schedule.

So if you state your subject clearly, your agenda item might read:

**To discuss the new sales brochure in the light of the budget and costings:**

- ▶ **format**
- ▶ **design**
- ▶ **content**
- ▶ **schedule.**

Now we're getting somewhere. Everyone can tell exactly what they are supposed to be discussing, and can prepare ideas or read background material accordingly. But there's more. We may all know what we're talking about, but where is the discussion leading?

**II** thinking fast

**SPEEDING BULLET**

If there are several points to discuss under one item, one of the fastest and clearest ways to indicate this on the agenda is to use bullet points.

Meetings aren't about open-ended discussions just for the fun of it. Who's got time for that? Certainly not you. They have to go somewhere, have a point, achieve something. But what? There are only three reasons why you should include an item on your agenda:

1 for information
2 for action
3 for decision.

Let's take a quick look at each of the three, and you should see how everything can fall into one of these categories.

INFORMATION

There is no point wasting everybody's time passing on information that can be circulated easily on paper. The only reason to bring up an information item at a meeting is if it needs to be passed on in person. This might be because:

- It needs clarifying or explaining, and people might need to ask questions for this purpose.

- It should come from a particular person.

- It has deep significance for the members of the meeting.

Progress reports on projects often need to be passed on at a meeting so that people can ask for clarification.

## ACTION

These items are usually preceded by at least some discussion. At the end of this, an action point determines what will happen next. There are all sorts of options, which might include:

- ▶ agreeing to find specific data to feed into the next meeting

- ▶ setting up another meeting or committee to deal with the matter in more depth and to report back

- ▶ taking specific action: anything from commissioning a designer, to cutting the confirmation time for online orders to ten minutes, to redesigning the delivery packaging so it's easier to open – you know the sort of thing that gets actioned in meetings.

## DECISION

This covers the matters that the meeting as a whole needs to decide. In a sense, many action points are delegated decision points – we all agree the policy, but someone else can take the decisions without wasting the meeting's time. But decision points are too important to delegate. They often start with a policy, but the meeting has to decide: 'How shall we implement this?' Often, you need to get the meeting to agree a decision for the psychological purpose of making everyone feel they have a stake in the decision.

So you will certainly need to discuss some items, but the discussion should leave you further on than you began. It is not just a vague conversation that leads nowhere. At the end of it you should make a decision or agree an action point to take the matter further.

*You* may know where each item is leading, but it's no good keeping it to yourself. State it on the agenda so everyone knows. You will find that this can lead to a slightly longer agenda: good. All the more information so everyone can prepare for the meeting thoroughly.

So your 'new brochure' agenda item will now look more like this:

**1: To discuss the new sales brochure in the light of the budget and costings:**

**For decision:**

 **format – number of pages/size/colours etc**

**For action:**

- ▶ **design – agree brief and invite designers to tender**
- ▶ **content – agree pitch (paper attached) and agree to brief writer**
- ▶ **schedule – discuss outline so schedule can be prepared.**

You may be wondering how you are supposed to find time to draw up this agenda. Well, don't worry, it really doesn't take long. You already have all the information, you're simply writing it all down. And, once you've done it, you've got your own notes, and the thought process functions as a valuable preparation. Writing a good agenda is all the preparation you need.

**thinkingsfast**

**TAKE NOTE**

You know what meetings you have coming up. So why not keep a sheet for making notes on each? As anything crops up, or thoughts occur to you, jot them down. Think about the odd agenda point while you're waiting for someone to answer the phone, or for your modem to connect. By the time you come to write the agenda, you should have most of the key items already jotted down along with the details you need to itemize on the agenda.

### ALLOCATING TIME

You're almost there. But there is just one more ingredient you need to add to create a thoroughly indispensible agenda. You need to allocate timings to each item. I know almost nobody else does it, but two wrongs don't make a right. If you can't waste time, you need to know how much time you aren't going to waste.

Suppose you have eight agenda items and you don't want this meeting to run over an hour (you haven't the time and there's no need for it), how are you going to make sure the first item doesn't take too long and squeeze others out? By working out how much time you can spare for each item, that's how.

It's no good simply dividing the hour into eight equal sections, obviously. It takes far longer to consider the proposal to integrate the sales and marketing functions than it does to agree the date of the next meeting. So allocate time on the basis of how long it:

**a** needs

**b** deserves.

Some relatively minor items genuinely take a few minutes to get through and, conversely, some important items don't actually need very long. But judge your timings on experience and common sense and make sure they add up to the total time you want to spend at this meeting.

Then write down your timings next to the agenda item, so everyone else can mentally prepare themselves for a meaty debate or a quick flit through the basics of the topic. The simplest way to do this is to write a start time next to each agenda item – it's also a quick way to check you're on course as the meeting progresses. So your finished agenda item now looks something like this:

**1: To discuss the new sales brochure in the light of the budget and costings: 10.35am**

**For decision:**

▶ **format – number of pages/size/colours etc**

**For action:**

▶ **design – agree brief and invite designers to tender**

▶ **content – agree pitch (paper attached) and agree to brief writer**

▶ **schedule – discuss outline so schedule can be prepared.**

And that's it. The art of writing a really effective, productive agenda. And the smart way to make sure everyone arrives at the meeting prepared for each item and knowing what to expect. So when it comes to running the meeting, you'll find that half the battle is won already.

## thinkingsfast

### PRUNING RAMBLERS

If you have someone at your meeting who is likely to ramble on about a particular pet topic, ask them in advance how long you should allow for it on the agenda, and steer them towards agreeing a sensible time. It makes it much easier to rein them in when it comes to it. You can even start by saying: 'Right, item 3. Robin and I both reckon we can cover this comfortably in ten minutes, don't we Robin?'

This is already the smartest way to write an agenda, and it's pretty fast too. But if you have the luxury of more time, it can be worth talking to one or two key people who will be at the meeting, if only to get them on your side.

There are always items that particular people feel they 'own'. They are in charge of the project in question or they are the acknowledged authority on the computer or on direct mail. Asking for their input when you prepare the agenda can be helpful in making it realistic, and it also makes the other person feel involved.

There are always items that particular people feel they 'own'

# 3 involving other people

To be honest, it's a bit late for this chapter if you have to go into the meeting in half an hour. But if you managed to take the advice in Chapter 1 to defer the meeting, you'll find the contents of this chapter valuable for saving time when you do finally hold the meeting.

Once you have prepared the agenda, you need to inform the other people who will attend the meeting. So the first thing to do is decide who will be there. Small meetings are always quicker, and often more productive, than large ones. This means that you want to include as few people as possible in this meeting. As a general guide:

▶ **The ideal number for a meeting is between four and seven.**

▶ **Up to ten people is manageable.**

▶ **Do whatever it takes to avoid meetings with over a dozen people – you'll be there all day.**

Now that's all very well, but it's not that easy dropping people from meetings. We all complain about meetings, but we hate being left out. People may feel they aren't thought important enough to be there or they may simply want the opportunity to put their case. Well, there are ways round these difficulties. The important thing is to keep in mind that you simply have to keep the numbers down because you haven't time for a big, unwieldy meeting. So here are a few ideas:

- Look through the agenda and see if some people can be scheduled to leave half way through the meeting or arrive in time for item 4 (another benefit of putting timings on the agenda). You don't want a constant traffic of people arriving and leaving, but the agenda will often split into two or even three sections very simply, and not everyone will need to be there for everything.

- An alternative to this is to hold two separate smaller meetings to cope with large numbers, just as we saw earlier for coping with an overlong agenda.

- Ask a small group to meet in advance and discuss certain items, and then ask just one representative from that meeting to attend yours and feed in any comments or proposals.

Having said all that, remember that there are times when the team needs to come together as a group in order to reinforce their identity as a team. Team briefings (which we'll look at in more detail later) can be larger, along with other meetings, where most items are for information rather than discussion leading to action or decision.

### TOO IMPORTANT FOR A MEETING

If people are likely to have their noses put out of joint by being excluded, call them in advance. Say: 'You're far too busy to come to this meeting; if I can pick your brains now for any comments or ideas we don't need to waste your time by dragging you along when you have more pressing things to do.'

PROVIDING BACK-UP

You've decided who you will include in this meeting, but before you circulate the agenda to them you need to add any supporting paperwork to it. Assuming you're normal, you probably find your stomach sinking at the thought of background papers. All those wodges of documents you know you won't have time to read.

### DEALING WITH DOCUMENTS

If ever you do find yourself without time to go through documents you should have read, you can still give the impression you've done your homework. Stick a few Post-it notes in the pages and make random underlinings and question marks in red ink in the margins.

If this has always been your private view of background papers, congratulations. Your instincts are right. Huge piles of documents with an agenda precariously balanced on top are, frankly, a stupid idea. Do you read them all from cover to cover? Of course you don't. And nor does anyone else.

Mind you, background papers circulated in advance do have some value, so we wouldn't want to abandon them completely:

▷ **It's better than everyone reading the papers in the meeting. You must have played that game – you all sit round in silence reading … and then waiting for the slowest person to catch up.**

▷ **It means people can think about the topic ahead of the meeting and come armed with useful comments or ideas.**

▷ **If anyone wants to add any data to what is already there, they have time to find the information before the meeting.**

**TECHNICAL PROBLEMS**

A few papers, such as financial or statistical documents, can be better presented at the meeting rather than in advance. They may need explanation or people might want to ask questions to clarify their meaning.

So if we don't want lots of paperwork, and we don't want no papers at all, the middle way should be clear. Short papers. Ask people to provide *brief* background papers, giving them as much advance notice as possible.

Once you have decided who to include in the meeting, and you have collected the necessary (short) background papers, you can circulate them with the agenda. And that's your preparation done.

## for next time

Make it a rule for your meetings that all background papers should be as brief as possible. If they run to any significant length, they should have a one-page summary attached. (Since this is all anyone is going to read, the rest of the paper might just as well be dropped.)

Sometimes you need to circulate a longer report or document; again, you should attach a brief summary if it is not already included. This should save a huge amount of time for you and everybody else, both before and during the meeting.

Ask people to provide brief background papers, giving them as much advance notice as possible

# 4 chairing the meeting

Let's get the worrying bit over with first. As a manager, you are judged on your results. Results only happen after action and decisions – which are the product of effective meetings. In other words, the effectiveness of your meetings will determine your results, and therefore your reputation.

There's no getting away from the fact that the success or failure of a meeting is down to the skills of whoever chairs it. However, this has a plus side: when the meeting is successful, everyone knows it is thanks to you (not that they will actually *say* thank you, mind). If your meetings achieve results, and achieve them fast, your reputation will be formidable.

Your preparation has already set you well down the path to a successful meeting. You already have:

▶ **a clear objective**

▶ **a detailed and useful agenda, stating what result to expect from each item and how long it will take**

⊳ only those people you really need, all well prepared with brief background papers where necessary.

Now you want to get through the meeting as fast as you can without cutting corners or leaving out anything important.

## STRUCTURE

The first thing to address is the way in which you tackle each agenda item. It's no good arriving at an item randomly from any direction, leaving some people wondering where it is coming from or where it is leading. You need to approach each item logically so that everyone in the meeting is clear about it. Some people may be deeply involved, while others haven't been concerned with the matter until now or know nothing of it at all.

So each item should be introduced. You can ask the person most responsible for it to do this or you can give an introduction yourself. Either way, the introduction should briefly cover:

1 why the item is on the agenda
2 a brief background to it up until this point
3 what needs to be established, proposed or decided at this meeting
4 the key arguments put forward so far on both sides of the issue
5 the possible courses of action this meeting could take.

### DOING THE INTRODUCTIONS

If someone else is responsible for a particular item, generally you would ask them to introduce it. However, if they are incapable of being brief you can always introduce it yourself – just find a way of doing it without putting their nose out of joint. It can also be wise for you to do the introduction for a controversial item, where neutrality is important. Otherwise, whichever side of the argument is represented in the introduction might appear to have your blessing.

The introduction should rarely take more than a minute or two and you should explain this to other members of the meeting – and demonstrate it by example. For instance, suppose the agenda item is the new sales brochure. You might introduce it by saying:

> We need a new sales brochure before the product launch in September, and we need to decide how best to spend what resources we have on it.
>
> The old brochure is out of date, and we get complaints that it isn't comprehensive enough.
>
> So we need to decide broadly how we can get the most out of the available budget.

*There is an argument that we should produce a lengthy and comprehensive brochure, even though this will mean a fairly simple and economical design. On the other hand, we could keep the main brochure short but glossy, and then back it up with a black and white catalogue listing of the more detailed product range.*

*So we need to decide whether we have one smart but simple brochure, or two brochures – one glossy and one fairly cheap black and white.*

*We also need to press on with the design and content, and outline a schedule so we can keep on top of the project.*

No doubt you can see that this brief introduction will occupy little time, but could save a great deal in the way of questions, confusion about the nature of the discussion and so on.

Once the introductions are over, there is a four-stage structure that will take you through the rest of the item without wasting time:

1 Examine the evidence.

2 Discuss the implications.

3 Arrive at a conclusion.

4 Form a decision.

***Examine the evidence.*** You need to go through all the relevant details that back up the arguments now. Anything substantial should have been circulated earlier so you don't have to waste time reading it all at the meeting. But you need to produce figures, costings, sample brochure styles, research results and so on – all the information necessary to carry the discussion forward.

***Discuss the implications.*** This is the real debate. All the evidence has been put before the meeting, so now is the time to invite views and arguments and discuss what it means.

***Arrive at a conclusion.*** Once everything that needs to be said has been, people are inclined to start repeating themselves if you let them. Once you sense that everything useful has been said, steer the team towards forming a consensus about what the best course of action is.

***Form a decision.*** Now summarize the conclusion and record it, along with any action points arising from it (we'll look at keeping minutes later in this chapter).

When it comes to your role in the chair, it's your job to make sure that the team follows this route through each agenda item. Keep reminding them what stage the meeting is at, whenever they start to stray. For example: 'Hang on, we haven't heard all the arguments yet so we can't start drawing conclusions' or 'We don't need to discuss the facts – we all know what they are. We need to move on and discuss their implications.'

 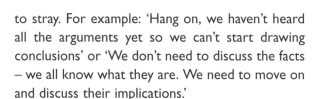

### WRITE IT UP

It can help to write up key questions on a flip chart or whiteboard – such as *What do these facts mean for us?* – in order to keep people on track.

You need to be firmly in control. Once you allow any kind of unhelpful behaviour – from intimidating to time-wasting – you invite everyone else to do it too. So don't permit the group to stray from the central purpose of the meeting. But don't wield an iron fist – unless it wears a velvet glove. In other words, be firm but don't intimidate people.

You may need to intervene occasionally to make sure that quieter members of the team get their chance to speak, or to invite a contribution from someone whose opinion you think would be valuable. Or you might want to summarize part way through a complex discussion if you sense confusion in the group.

## RABBIT, RABBIT, RABBIT

One of the toughest challenges when you want to keep things brief is handling someone who is naturally garrulous. The thing to remember if you want to stop the flow is: take the wheel; don't try to stand in front of the car. Pick up on a remark and use it to move the discussion on. For example: 'That's a very good point, Jim, and worth thinking about. What do you reckon, Brenda? Have we got enough staff to cover a three-day exhibition?'

You don't want to waste time here, but if you have a sensible agenda and you stay in control, you should be able to keep the meeting running on time without any sense of rush or people being bulldozed into making decisions before they feel ready.

KEEPING TO TIME ...

... which brings us to another key part of your job. You don't want to bulldoze people, but you certainly don't want to waste their time either. You need to crack on with your meeting and create an atmosphere of urgency without rushing.

The first step towards this is to make sure your meetings start on time. Don't you hate hanging around for ten minutes at the start of every meeting while people turn up? The solution is simple: just start your meeting on time (of course, you have to set the example). If anyone isn't there, they will miss out on the chance to contribute. And don't go back over the first part of the meeting when they finally turn up: they'll find out what happened when they read the minutes. It won't take long before everyone learns to turn up to your meetings promptly.

Another popular form of time-wasting is for people to give long briefings or try to circulate papers at meetings, simply because they didn't get their act together to circulate the information with the agenda. Don't stand for it. Unless they have a very good reason, such as an item that had to be added late, make them wait until the next meeting to have their topic discussed. That'll learn 'em.

### LATE ARRIVALS

Record on the minutes of each meeting anyone who arrived late or left early. Ostensibly, you are recording who was present for any decision or discussion. But in fact it will help to shame people into turning up on time.

**TURNING THE TABLES ON TIME-WASTERS**

If you know your meeting is likely to be plagued by timewasters, schedule it for an hour before lunch, or at 4.30 pm. Few people are eager to procrastinate if it's going to cut into their personal time.

As far as the general course of the meeting is concerned, you can encourage people to keep to time by various means:

- ▶ **Get them to stick to the point.** If you never allow digressions and amusing but barely relevant anecdotes, people will stop trying to insert them into your meetings. Be consistent and it will get easier all the time. By the way, that's not to say you shouldn't allow humour, which can be invaluable at meetings; just don't allow it to ramble off the point.

- ▶ Remind them of the time: 'We've only got ten minutes for this item, so we need to move towards a conclusion'.

- ▶ If your own contributions are concise and relevant, people will follow your lead (not every time, but broadly speaking).

- ▶ Adopt a dynamic, urgent tone of voice to show that you want to crack on.

- Hurry people along with your body language: lean forward, make eye contact with the speaker, raise your eyebrows, and nod quickly to indicate when a point has been made.

You can also make sure that each agenda item reaches the intended conclusion or, if it can't do so for any reason, abandon it swiftly and get on with the rest of the meeting. The kind of indicators that an item should be abandoned include:

- You don't have all the facts you need to reach a conclusion.

- You need input from people who aren't here.

- Everyone needs more time to think and to discuss the subject with other colleagues.

- Things are changing in a way that may negate any decision you make now.

- You don't have time to do the subject justice at this meeting.

- It is clear that this matter can be settled more quickly and more effectively outside the meeting.

In any of these cases, you should close the item and move on, but make sure that the necessary action is taken to keep the matter moving – agree what facts will be circulated before the next meeting, set up another meeting or whatever.

**WRITING BY COMMITTEE**

A common time-wasting factor in meetings is discussions of papers that degenerate into a general redrafting of the paper by committee. If you spot this happening, get everyone to agree what the problems with the paper are and then delegate someone to do a fresh draft later and circulate it.

MINUTES

Your whole meeting will be a waste of time if everyone leaves at the end of it and nothing happens. Perhaps they all thought someone else was going to take action. Maybe they didn't realize that a final decision had been reached. It is essential that there is no room for doubt about what happened at the meeting and what is going to happen next. That's what minutes are all about.

# thinking smart

## BEYOND REASONABLE DOUBT

If there is any room for doubt or argument, you can read out the minutes as you write them at the end of an agenda item and check everyone is in agreement.

Whoever actually writes down the minutes, *you* are responsible for them. They don't have to be lengthy, but they must be clear. They should include:

- the time, date and place of the meeting, and who chaired it
- the names of those who were present and apologies for absence – and names and times for those who arrived late or left early
- each agenda item discussed. For each item the minutes should state key arguments, decisions or action points, and the name of the person responsible for carrying out the action points
- the time the meeting ended
- the date, time and place of the next meeting.

Your whole meeting will be a waste of time if everyone leaves at the end of it and nothing happens

## thinking fast

### SETTING A DATE

It is generally much quicker to get your diaries out at the end of a meeting and set the next date (assuming it isn't a regular meeting), rather than spend ages back and forth on the phone fixing it up later.

Running meetings faster and more productively doesn't take any longer than running them unproductively – in fact, of course, it's quicker. So you can get it right this time as well as next time.

But there are ground rules that you can follow for all the next times to make sure that it gets easier and easier to hold fast, effective meetings. Once your team gets to know your style, they will adapt to it naturally. And the more consistent it is, the sooner and the better they will get to know it. So to keep your meetings swift be consistent about:

- ▶ starting every meeting on time, whether or not everyone has arrived
- ▶ keeping the introductions to agenda items as brief as you can
- ▶ discouraging digression
- ▶ insisting that papers are circulated in advance (unless they accompany a late agenda item)
- ▶ keeping your own contributions brief and to the point.

Keep your own contributions brief and to the point

# 5 handling people

We've already covered everything you need to know about running meetings ... so long as everyone who attends your meetings is permanently affable, amenable, confident and co-operative. However, if you never have to handle any conflict, aggression or domineering behaviour in any of your meetings, I can only assume you work for a Trappist order.

If you are living in the real world with the rest of us, you are going to need to know how to handle people if you want to keep your meetings fast and effective. Some meetings will go smoothly, but others will test your skills to the limit. If you can't stay well in control the meeting will degenerate, take far longer than it needs to, and achieve less. Worse still, it may leave behind resentment and ill feeling in the team. So people skills are vital to chairing meetings productively.

## SERVANT NOT MASTER

You may be the most senior person at the meeting, but your function while you are chairing it is to be the servant of the team. It is not your job to pull rank, impose decisions, give opinions or wield power. If you do this, you will have a seriously detrimental effect on the meeting:

- ▶ You will intimidate less confident people, who may be put off making comments or proposing ideas that could have been useful.

- ▶ People will not offer opinions if they think they will be shouted down or made to feel foolish.

- ▶ The team members will not feel a shared responsibility for decisions that they feel were imposed on them.

You are there to make sure the meeting achieves its aims. You should:

- ▶ Maintain the focus of the group.

- ▶ Explain and clarify where necessary.

- ▶ Keep the discussion moving towards a resolution in the shortest reasonable time.

- ▶ Remain neutral.

Whoa there! Remain *neutral*? You're the boss and you're supposed to let decisions go through without even expressing an opinion? That can't be right, surely.

But it *is* right, and it's very important. Think about it for a moment. Your interests are the interests of the group and it is essential, for a free flow of ideas and opinions, that you are seen to be on everybody's side. That way, you can be seen to be fair and the task of keeping discipline becomes much easier. You are the servant of the group – you simply want the meeting to reach the best decision.

What's more, if you give an opinion – especially early on – it can deter junior members from expressing a contradictory view for fear of arguing with the boss. Not only should they feel able to say how they feel, there is also a good chance that they have an important point to make that is worth hearing.

And what about your opinion? Well, someone else is almost bound to share it and they will express it for you without the meeting having to know how you feel. Then, assuming the debate hasn't changed your view, you can sum up in favour of the colleague who expresses your opinion.

THE GROUND RULES

One of the advantages of team meetings is that everyone knows everyone else, and the meetings

### MAKING YOUR CASE

If there is a danger that your views might not be expressed as well as you would like, or that certain arguments might be omitted, have a private word with a like-minded colleague before the meeting. Make sure they will express the points you want made, and furnish them with any useful arguments they might need.

are probably regular and certainly fairly frequent. So if you can set up a clear meeting style from the start, people will learn to stick to it without being told. Of course, this isn't much use for today's meeting, or tomorrow's, but you can start laying down the ground rules now. In a short time you should start to see the results in easier, pleasanter and quicker meetings.

You need to spell out the ground rules so that everyone is clear about them. Disagreements are fine – indeed they are often necessary to find the best course of action – but they should never become personal or unpleasant. To make sure your meetings follow this principle, you need to foster a sense of respect for the meeting and everyone in it. So set out four 'rules' for everyone in the team to follow:

**You need to spell out the groundrules so that everyone is clear about them**

1 Always ask for clarification if anything is unclear.

2 Conversely, always be willing to give explanations or answer questions for other members of the meeting.

3 Everyone can help to encourage quieter members of the team to have their say and keep the more dominant members in check.

4 Team members should listen to each other and treat every idea with respect even if they disagree with it.

## HANDLING AGGRESSION

Disagreements can be a healthy way to force new ideas out and often lead to even better solutions. Trouble is, people can become emotionally involved and rational disagreement quickly changes to aggressive argument. Sometimes people become very attached to their own ideas and don't want to see them rejected or they feel they are being personally criticized. Sometimes a certain decision will cause extra work or problems for them so they argue heatedly against it.

From your point of view this is unproductive and a waste of precious time. And you want to keep relations in your team on good terms both in and out of meetings. So you need to find ways to make sure that strong feelings are kept in harness and that the meeting doesn't become unpleasant.

Ideally, you should be able to spot trouble brewing and stop it before it starts. It is much easier to keep the peace than to regain it once it has been lost. So as soon as the mood starts to heat up, take action. Respond to the first personal snipe you hear with: 'Let's not get personal. We're not discussing what went wrong last time. We need to decide what lead times we need on this contract.'

There is a four-stage process for bringing overheated discussions back off the boil and keeping the meeting moving forward in the process:

1 Let people let off steam.

2 Be neutral.

3 Involve the rest of the group.

4 Keep to the facts.

The sooner you bring these techniques into play when you see trouble brewing, the less heated things will get.

*Let people let off steam*

The first principle is that once strong feelings are aroused, it is counterproductive to attempt to repress them. You know yourself that if you are angry and someone tells you to calm down, it just makes you want to clout them. And the thing that irritates most of all is feeling that no one is listening.

So as soon as you sense heated emotions, ask the person concerned to express them. This opportunity to let off steam will help them feel that the group is at least listening to them, and will enable them to calm down by themselves. Ask what's wrong and insist that the rest of the team listens without interrupting for a few moments, until the person has got their feelings out in the open.

Of course, you don't want a fight to develop. If you feel this is a danger, come down firmly on any

**thinking smart**

### GET THE FEELING

It isn't only aggression that you need to be on the lookout for. If someone is sulking or withdrawing you need to recognize this, and handle it in the same way. Use the word 'feel' rather than 'think', to encourage them to express their feelings. So you might say: 'I sense you're not feeling happy about this. What's the trouble?'

remarks that are getting personal, and don't allow this sort of bickering or arguing to start. You can intervene and let each person have their say in turn, but get them to speak through you rather than directly to each other until tempers begin to cool.

Once people have had their say and got their aggression out of their system, they tend to calm down by themselves. When angry they will often be pigheaded, but once they are calmer it is easier to get them to listen to rational argument and to express their own point of view more reasonably.

### Be neutral

We've already looked at the need to be neutral yourself, and this is never more important than when feelings are running high. It is essential that you are seen to be on no one's side but the group's as a whole. Your focus is on resolving the debate amicably and sensibly, and without wasting time on it. So whatever you do:

▶ Avoid getting drawn into the argument.

▶ Don't start allocating blame.

▶ Don't criticize anyone for having strong feelings – they are entitled to them so long as they express them without getting personal.

▶ Don't lose your cool, or you will also lose credibility and respect.

As soon as you sense heated emotions, ask the person concerned to express them

### YOU'VE GOT TO LAUGH

Humour is one of the best tools for restoring calm and good relations, and the opportunity to laugh can act as a safety valve for everyone, not only those who are at the centre of the argument. Just make sure the laugh is not at the expense of anyone at the meeting.

There are times when someone's behaviour at a meeting really is out of line, of course. No matter what the provocation, it isn't on to threaten violence or to be deeply personal. But if one of your team deserves to be pulled up for this kind of behaviour, do it later and in private. Giving them a dressing down in front of the meeting will only increase their anger, as well as being thoroughly unprofessional.

*Involve the rest of the group*

When two angry people lock horns, they often lose sight of what is going on around them. One of the best techniques for diluting their emotions is simply to bring other people in to the debate. Of course, if you ask other people just to stick in their twopenny worth you are simply encouraging the argument to expand and dragging in the rest of the team.

The trick is to change the subject subtly. Keep to the same topic, but ask someone else for a new angle on it. Look for something that will move the discussion on (you're still working to the deadline of whatever finish time you specified, don't forget). You want to add new facts, bring in a new perspective or shed light on the cause of the problem.

Suppose the argument is about whether the new brochures should be delayed to incorporate the new autumn product range or whether they should be ready in time for the May mailshot. You could bring in someone else by saying, for example:

-  Ellen, you've been involved in this for four or five years now. What has happened in the past?

- Tom, would it be possible to get the brochure out by May?

- Hilary, how about giving the new products their own supplementary brochure? That's what you used to do at your last company isn't it?

The aim here is not to shut out the warring parties, but simply to calm them down. Even angry people can have a valid point to make, and they may well be right. So don't exclude their point of view; just give them some time to relax and calm down while others are speaking.

*Keep to the facts*

This technique is another useful way to keep tempers from flaring. If people express their opinions, they are bound to take sides in some way, whether they want to or not. So avoid opinions and stick to facts. They are much harder to argue with. Ask questions such as: 'What have we done about this in the past?' or 'How much more would two brochures cost?' If anyone tries to respond with an opinion, simply say 'Let's stick to facts for the moment …' and then repeat the question.

## CONTROL THE DOMINANT TENDENCY

One of the other key people problems you may encounter at your meetings is the dominant people who are inclined to squash the weaker members of the team. This isn't necessarily an aggressive urge at all. It's just that some people are naturally confident and garrulous while others aren't. And some of the more confident people aren't necessarily considering the opinions of those who aren't prepared to butt in. You, on the other hand, *should* be considering them. But what is the best way to handle them?

You need a two-pronged approach. First, you need to keep the bigger personalities in check. And second, you must encourage the quieter ones to speak out. It's not too difficult: the important thing is to notice when it needs doing. If you spot anyone trying to speak you can say: 'Hold on a minute, Ellen. Hilary, did you want to say something?' Let the dominant members of the group have their say, but then create a space for the others to comment too. (Don't try to force an input from people who have nothing to say, however, or you will simply intimidate them.) The one thing to look out for here is that you shouldn't take sides, as we know – and that includes not seeming to side with the weaker members of the meeting.

If you need to use more forceful methods, here are some tips:

- Go round the meeting occasionally and ask each person in turn to say what they think. People generally co-operate with this slightly more formal process and keep quiet while others speak.

- If some people are intimidated because they are juniors and don't like to disagree with the more senior members of the team, ask them to give their opinion first, before you ask the more senior people.

- Have a rule that no one can either interrupt or disagree unless they first summarize what the previous speaker has said. This ensures everyone listens properly, preserves clarity, and it slows the faster ones down.

thhfhhthisfsfg

> ### GET IT IN WRITING
>
> If your team includes people who tend to dominate by repeating their ideas endlessly, record all ideas on a flip chart or a board. Once it's on display they will be reassured that they don't need to repeat it again. And you can save time and get on with the meeting.

## BE POSITIVE

One of the biggest dangers in running meetings is that you will get through the whole agenda in the allocated time, with all the decisions and action points you needed, but ... they are not the best decisions and action points.

When time is tight, it is especially crucial that you reach the *best* decisions. You can't afford to be unproductive, and you have to live with these decisions. You don't have time in your life to go back over the meeting in six months' time looking for a better way or clearing up the mess created by a wrong decision.

There are three key rules for making sure your meetings arrive at the best decisions:

1 Set the right tone.
2 Don't settle for the first solution.
3 Be creative.

*Set the right tone*

You've been at enough meetings to recognize this one. How often do meetings become focused on the negative points, the problems, the difficulties? Is there even a decent solution at all? People are happy to pick holes in each other's ideas, without putting forward any viable alternatives of their own.

Staying positive is largely down to the mood you create in the meeting. Make it clear that there is always a good solution, and it can be found if everyone looks for it. Encourage new ideas – even if they don't seem particularly promising – and keep the enthusiasm going with positive remarks: 'We can certainly build on that,' 'Good thinking' or 'I'm sure we can find a way round this.'

You will also need to keep negativity to a minimum. Some people are naturally cautious and that's fine – in fact, without them the rest of us

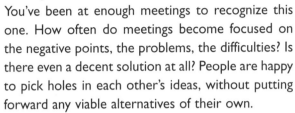

## THE POWER OF POSITIVE THINKING

If the team seems negative about the existence of a good solution, remind them of what Henry Ford said on the subject: 'Whether you believe you can or whether you believe you can't: you're absolutely right.'

would get into a lot of trouble. But don't allow hole picking for the sake of it. Negative remarks should have a relevant and useful point.

Once an idea has been rejected, don't allow further debate on it. There isn't time and it will damage the mood of the meeting. So don't allow comments such as: 'I'll tell you another reason why it wouldn't work …'

### Don't settle for the first solution

There's a Woody Allen film in which someone says: 'I know the answer!' and relates it. Allen replies: 'That's not *the* answer; it's *an* answer. And it's the wrong answer.' Just because a solution fits, it doesn't make it the only one or even the best one. But often a meeting will reach one possible solution and then stop looking.

thinking fast

#### SEE IF YOU CAN DO ANY BETTER

If you are cursed with a negative bunch of people on your team, you could institute a rule that no one is allowed to say no to an idea unless they have a better alternative to offer. If this is too constricting, just bring the rule into play when you sense that the meeting is being dragged down.

For example, in the case of those brochures, you might decide that you should have a single brochure for now and add a second brochure for the new products in the autumn. But if you continued to look for better ideas, you might have found one. How about a short run of brochures for now and extra pages stapled into the centre for the next print run?

That's all very nice in theory, but how can you tell when you've got to the end of the possible solutions? After all, you haven't got time to keep the discussion going indefinitely on the off chance there's a better solution somewhere if you can only hit on it.

The answer is that you can rarely know for certain, but you can know that you've given it your best shot. A positive atmosphere is a good start, but there are other techniques too:

Just because a solution fits, it doesn't make it the only one

- Encourage ideas from everyone; don't let one person shout down the others.

- Record all ideas and suggestions on a flip chart or a board. This encourages positive thinking – you can all see where you're getting to. People want to see their ideas written up, and they can use other suggestions as a springboard for their own ideas.

- Go round the group every so often, asking for positive ideas and suggestions.

The core principle behind all these techniques is the same: the more solutions you can come up with, the less chance you have of omitting the best one.

*Be creative*

Clearly, if you want people to come up with useful ideas and suggestions, you are asking them to be creative. Contrary to popular belief, we are all capable of being creative, but most of us need encouragement to do it. That's *your* job.

The way to generate good ideas is to create lots of ideas. The most famously creative people in history, from Archimedes to Einstein, didn't have a much higher hit rate of good ideas than the rest of us. They were simply prolific. If every tenth idea is a good one, and every fiftieth idea is a great one, a meeting that generates a hundred ideas has a better chance than one that generates only five ideas. It really is that simple. So to encourage a hundred ideas instead of five:

- Allow all suggestions, however unpromising – they may be the jumping-off point for a great idea.

- Record all ideas on a flip chart so others can build on them.

- Don't allow anyone's ideas to be criticised or put down – it will discourage people from volunteering any more suggestions.

- Encourage people to be wacky, bizarre and adventurous in their ideas.
- Accord each idea the same value.
- As always, you should remain neutral and not be seen to favour any ideas over any others.

Once the ideas seem to have dried up, you can pick out the most promising by finding the ones with the most positive points in their favour – no need to get picky and negative about any ideas that are rejected. Look at all the most positive ideas before making a final selection.

## REACHING CONSENSUS

When it comes to taking decisions at a team meeting, you are generally looking for a consensus – at least for any decision of importance. You want everyone in the team to buy into this decision and share responsibility for seeing it through, so everyone has to agree to it. In other words, you need to reach a consensus.

There is a popular misconception that a consensus decision is one that everyone has voted for unanimously. If this were true, it is hard to see how most decisions could get made at all. However, insisting on a consensus decision avoids going with a majority decision in which the minority is strongly in disagreement. If you did this, you would have a small faction within the team that did not feel committed to the decision.

No, what you need is a consensus – a decision that, while not necessarily everyone's first choice, is nevertheless acceptable to the whole team. A decision everyone can live with, even if it's not what they really wanted. If you explain the value of a consensus to your team – that no one has to abide by a decision they fundamentally disagree with – you'll be surprised to find that they will manage to arrive at one.

## for next time

The techniques in this chapter are as easy to implement when you're under time pressure as when you aren't. In fact, under pressure is when you need them most. But some of them take a little more practice than others.

Handling difficult people at meetings is an invaluable skill. Start by learning how to handle the difficult types you already have on your team. If you know all your meetings are attended by a prima donna, a whinger or a cynical sniper, begin by learning what you can do to curtail these people's more negative characteristics. You might want to read one of the companion volumes to this one: *Fast Thinking: Difficult People*.

Another area where you can develop your skills to make your meetings more productive without being any longer is creative thinking. If you can teach your team to be creative in meetings, you'll find there's a knock-on effect and they will become more creative outside meetings too. Before you know it, you could have an explosion of ideas and brainwaves around your department.

There are numerous creative techniques you can usefully employ at meetings, from brainstorming (as we saw earlier) to Edward de Bono's six thinking hats. They make meetings both fun and hugely productive, and could earn you quite a reputation if you use them regularly. Buy a book on business creativity and start feeding some new techniques into your meetings – now there's an idea.

**What you need is a consensus – a decision that, while not necessarily everyone's first choice, is nevertheless acceptable to the whole team**

# 6 the type of meeting

All the guidelines we've looked at so far are generic ones for running team meetings. But certain types of team meetings have specific guidelines attached. Running a team briefing session, for example, is not exactly the same as running a project meeting. So this chapter provides a rundown of what you need to know for the most common types of team meeting, for example:

- ▶ **regular departmental meetings**
- ▶ **inter-departmental meetings**
- ▶ **project meetings**
- ▶ **team briefing sessions.**

If you're rushed, just read the one that applies to you now. You can still come back later and read the rest of them.

The key thing about regular departmental meetings (you know, the Monday morning one or whatever it is in your case) is that it is the only time the department really exists except on paper. The rest of the time people are working in ones, twos and threes. This is their chance to come together as a team and reinforce their group identity. So this is your chance to cultivate real team spirit. This means you want the meetings to be as upbeat and unifying as you can manage.

The biggest threat to this is the status battle. When the whole team is together, many people see it as a golden opportunity to assert their position in the hierarchy. This can lead to point-scoring and even battles for supremacy over certain issues. What you want to do, however, is to ensure that while ideas can clash, people don't.

Your neutrality, of course, is all important. But neutrality doesn't have to be silent – it can show favour so long as it is equal. When people are battling for status and position in the hierarchy, it is your approval they seek. So make them all feel they're doing OK. Cool down arguments before they get out of hand with interventions such as: 'You've got a good point there, Charlie, but Ellen is quite right that delivery times should be a higher priority.'

Ideas should clash, but not people

**KEEP IT SHORT**

One of the chief mistakes people make when they chair departmental meetings is to put too many items on the agenda. Specifically, they tend to include items that only concern one or two people there. Since you can't afford to waste time in meetings, make sure these items are addressed outside the meeting. Informal chats or smaller meetings, with or without you, can take care of a lot of items and free up everyone's time.

*Why are we here?*

A common danger at departmental meetings is that they become repetitive, drawing on old agendas for a list of this week's or this month's items. It is easy to forget the real function of the department – which goes back to your original objective. So make a point of livening up the meeting, and reinforcing the real focus of the team, by adding 'why are we here?' items (unless the agenda is really packed this week).

Look at the big issues. Why are delivery times so slow? Why are we losing a lot of new customers? Don't get bogged down in overtime staffing issues and machine repair updates. You may get some invaluable ideas, people will feel involved in the stuff that really counts, and they will be reminded why they are there.

### INTER-DEPARTMENTAL MEETINGS

The biggest problem you tend to face at inter-departmental meetings is turf wars. Each department head fighting their own corner. Department heads, what's more, tend to be pretty confident types, and you can end up with a roomful of them slugging it out. But more often, there are two key combatants – at least at any given time. Marketing is always sniping at distribution perhaps,

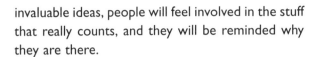
thinking smart

#### WATCH THE COSTS

Meetings are expensive, but few people realize how expensive. It is easy to calculate the cost of a regular team meeting such as this, and it's highly illuminating. Once you have done the sums, you can apply them every time. Calculate the cost of each person's time – you know their salaries – and then add the lost income they could have been earning if they hadn't been in the meeting: missed sales, uncompleted units in production or whatever. Your meeting could easily be costing hundreds of pounds, perhaps even thousands, an hour.

or accounts and personnel are frozen into a permanent cold war.

You can't expect to bring universal peace and the end of all conflict – nor should you. The problem arises from people's genuine loyalty to their own team. So what can you do to keep the meeting productive and reasonably good-natured? Well, here are a few tips:

- If you know there will be conflict, call the two parties privately in advance. Say to one: 'This is a sensible plan, but it's going to give marketing some problems. Can you think about ways to ease things for them?' When you call the marketing manager you might say: 'This is a problem for you, I can see. But it will be a huge improvement for distribution. I'd like you to consider whether there isn't a compromise that would suit you both.'

- If two members of the inter-departmental team really are at loggerheads, ask them to get together and come back to the next meeting with a joint recommendation (that should make them think twice next time they want a barney at one of your meetings).

- Use any opportunity to unite the team by talking about threats from outside – competitors, worrying new legislation, recession, the strength of the pound or some other collective worry. Schedule these kinds of items to follow divisive issues so you can reunite the group.

### CONGRATULATIONS!

There are all sorts of undercurrents at meetings, of course, and especially inter-departmental ones. Everyone will be vying for your approbation, so use meetings to congratulate people publicly on their contributions. 'Pete, that idea of yours about improving call-out times has already cut call-out complaints by 45 per cent. Well done.' You don't have to congratulate each person the same number of times, but make sure you are fair about what earns praise and about who gets it.

PROJECT MEETINGS

Project meetings are, by their nature, very focused. There may be many different aspects of the project to discuss, but they are still limited to the range of the project itself. You need to keep the enthusiasm for the project high and keep everyone working to deadlines, so the mood of the meeting should be positive and upbeat with a sense of urgency about it (good news if you want to spend as little time as possible in meetings).

Project meetings require discipline, both about the meeting and the project itself:

- ▶ Discipline about the meeting is essential. Project meetings are all about checking budgets, schedules, quality and problems. And about ironing out snags. So don't let the meeting wander off the point. Keep it very focused, and focused on the future. This isn't the place to hold post-mortems into why we are behind schedule; just concentrate on how to get back on course. The past is important only in as much as it sheds light on the future. If understanding why the schedule slipped helps prevent it recurring, fine. But don't start making recriminations and allocating blame.

- ▶ Discipline about the project means that once it is under way, you should stick with your plan. It can be very tempting to change things because someone has a great idea about doing things differently. But this is how projects go off course and get behind schedule. Unless there is a really exceptional reason to change, don't.

**thinking smart**

### BLURRING THE LINES

Try handing over chairing your project meetings – or parts of them – to different members of the team. The nature of project teams is such that everyone needs to work for the team as a whole, rather than focus on working just for their immediate boss. Hierarchies can get in the way of this. A junior member of the department may be in charge of part of the project in which they have authority over more senior members. So it can help to blur the traditional lines of command.

## TEAM BRIEFING SESSIONS

One of the most successful approaches to communication within organizations is team briefing, a system pioneered by The Industrial Society. If you don't already hold team briefings, it is a good idea to introduce them (just as soon as you have the time). They are unlike other team meetings because all the items are for information only, not for decision. So the best news of all is that you don't have to get your act together to circulate an agenda in advance.

The overall approach ideally involves the whole company, led from the top down, in which all team leaders are briefed and, in turn, brief their own teams. If your team is part of a larger organization that doesn't operate team briefing, you would do well to recommend it. In the meantime you can still operate a reduced system with your own team, even without the support of top management.

The principles behind team briefing are:

▶ **People cannot co-operate fully unless they know what's going on.**

▶ **The best way to bond a group of people into a team is to talk to them as a team, about team concerns.**

▶ **The fact that you are the one doing the briefing strengthens your position and demonstrates in an effective but non-confrontational way that you are in charge.**

In order for team briefing to work effectively, The Industrial Society has identified five rules to which you must adhere. The briefing sessions need to be:

1 face-to-face
2 in small teams of between 4 and 15 people
3 run by the team leader
4 regular (preferably monthly or thereabouts)
5 relevant to the team.

*Monitoring*

If your team is part of a larger briefing system, or if there are teams within your team that have their own briefings, there is a sixth rule: briefings should be monitored. This means that if you brief several senior members of your team who go on to brief their own teams, you need to:

▶ **Check any information they are adding to your brief, that is 'local' to their own team.**

▶ **Sit in on their briefing sessions from time to time (but as an observer *only*).**

▶ **Make occasional random checks with members of their team to see how effective their briefing has been.**

These precautions should ensure that the system remains effective and that no misunderstandings or Chinese whispers work their way into the system.

*The briefing*

Team briefing sessions should last for about half an hour. The Industrial Society recommends that you have four categories of information on which you brief your team – the four 'P's:

1 **Progress.** Give the team performance results. Did they meet last month's targets? How do they compare with other teams in the organization or with competitors? What new orders have there been? Any special successes or failures? Has the competition brought out any new products?

2 **Policy.** This section covers any changes in systems, new deadlines, holiday arrangements, new legislation affecting the team, training courses, pensions and so on.

3 **People.** New team members, members leaving (including why and where they're going), new MD or senior management, changes in other departments that the team deals with, promotions (including why), overtime, relocation, absenteeism, exhibition stand staffing and so on.

4 **Points for action.** Practical information such as new security measures that must be taken, suggestion schemes, maintenance priorities,

correcting rumours, housekeeping details and the like.

A brief is just that – a brief; it's not a discussion. You have set (though not circulated) your agenda in advance and you should work through it:

- ▶ **Encourage questions, but not debate. If people want fuller information, explanations or reasons you should try to help, but don't get into arguments. If you feel an argument brewing, explain that this is not the time for it but you are happy for team members to raise the issue another time.**

- ▶ **Encourage comments and suggestions and note them down, but don't discuss them now. You can arrange an individual or team session for that later, if necessary.**

- ▶ **If anyone asks you something you don't know, find it out for them in the next day or two.**

thinking fast

ONGOING FILE

Rather than sit down before the briefing session and agonize over what you might have left off your agenda, it makes sense to have a file where you continually put notes or papers for the next team briefing. When you come to prepare, you should find everything in there – a much quicker way to prepare and you make sure your agenda is comprehensive.

- ▶ Check that team members have understood anything complicated by asking questions to make sure it's clear to them.

- ▶ Summarise the key points at the end of the briefing.

- ▶ Find something positive to finish with so that people leave on an upbeat.

- ▶ Don't run over time – 30 minutes should be ample.

- ▶ Give the date of the next briefing so that everyone can mark it in their diary and make sure they are available.

- ▶ If anyone is absent from the briefing session, brief them yourself when they return.

Like all team meetings, team briefing not only deals with the items on the agenda, it also cements the group and reinforces your position at the head of it.

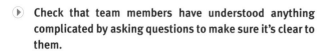

## for next time

Think about the type of team meeting you're holding, and what particular type of handling it calls for. Take into account the personalities at the meeting, and spend a little time thinking about likely conflicts and the best ways to handle them. Once you can run fast and productive team meetings, your reputation will rocket and – best of all – your diary may even begin to have empty spaces in it (only joking).

A brief is just that. It's not a discussion

# team meeting in ten minutes

Whoops! Ten minutes to zero hour and you still haven't started planning your meeting. Your best bet is to phone round and put it off for an hour – or better still cancel it. But that isn't always possible. In that case, you'd better stick to the essentials. That's all you have time for.

Since you're reading this book, you clearly want the odd tip. So here goes:

- ▶ Read the first bit of Chapter 1 (pages 8–11) so you know how to set an objective. I know you think it's a waste of time but you haven't got time to argue, so just do it.

- ▶ On your word processor, put down a list of items you think should be on the agenda.

- Check this list against your objective. If any item doesn't help further your objective, it doesn't belong on the agenda. Get rid of it.

- Now delete anything that can wait until your next meeting or be handled outside the meeting – by you or by anybody else (but make a note somewhere so it doesn't get forgotten permanently).

- Now you should have the shortest possible agenda. It doesn't matter how short it is – when was the last time you heard anyone complain that a meeting hadn't gone on long enough?

- Now knock the list into some kind of order. Urgent items first. Items that require the team to be awake and creative near the top of the agenda. Keep items in logical groups. And don't try to discuss anything that depends on the outcome of an item you haven't got to yet.

- Now read the bit of Chapter 2 about adding detail to the agenda (pages 22 to 27). Use any remaining time to do this. Include the particular aspects of each item you want to cover and also state whether this agenda item is for information, action or decision.

- Print off a copy of this agenda for everyone at the meeting. It may be rushed and not circulated in advance, but it'll still knock spots off most agendas.

When was the last time you heard anyone complain that a meeting hadn't gone on long enough?